Things to make and do for Christmas

Fiona Watt and Ray Gibson

Designed by Joe Pedley and Non Figg
Illustrated by Amanda Barlow
Cover design by Katrina Fearn
Photographs by Howard Allman
Additional illustrations by Nicola Butler, Chris Chaisty and Nelupa Hussain

There are lots of Christmas stickers in the middle of the book.
You can use them to decorate the things you make from this book,
or to decorate cards, presents and decorations of your own.

Glittery shapes	2	Christmas stockings	12	Christmas beads	22
Polar bear pop-up card	4	Advent calendar	14	Paper angels	24
Tree and snowflake	6	Fingerprint fat robins	16	Printed penguins	26
decorations		Tree card	17	Handprinted angel	28
Reindeer wrapping paper	8	Gift tags	18	Wrapping ideas	30
Snowman paperchain	10	Wrapping paper	20	Star card	32

Make lots of decorations using different shapes of cookie cutters.

Glittering shapes

1. Press a big cookie cutter firmly into a slice of white bread.

2. Push the bread shape out of the cutter very carefully.

3. Press the end of a straw into the shape to make a hole.

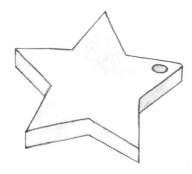

4. Put the bread shape onto a baking rack. Leave it overnight. It will get hard.

5. Mix a little paint with household glue (PVA). Paint around the edges of the shape.

6. Paint the top of the shape. When it is dry, turn it over and paint the other side.

These bread shapes are for decoration only. Do not eat them.

Hang these on your Christmas tree or use them as hanging decorations.

7. Glue lots of glitter onto the top of the shape. Add sequins and tiny beads, too.

8. Push a long piece of thread through the hole. Make a loop at the end of the thread.

9. Push the ends of the thread through the loop. Make a knot and pull it tight.

Polar bear pop-up card

The pieces of paper should be the same size.

Keep the paper folded as you cut.

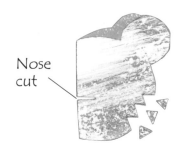

Nose cut

1. Fold a piece of white paper in half. Do the same with a piece of blue paper.

2. On the white paper, draw half of a bear's head against the fold, like this.

3. Cut around the head. Make a cut for a nose. Cut out shapes along the edge for fur, too.

The polar bear pops up in the middle of the card. You'll need to decorate the front too.

Follow the steps on page 18 for a glitter star.

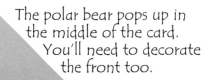

4. Lift the nose and fold it flat onto the front, like this. Crease the fold. Fold it behind, too.

5. Open out the head. Push a finger through the nose from the back, so that it stands up.

Press on a sticker from the sticker pages.

Glue on a paper shape (see page 6). Dab on thick white paint for snow. Sprinkle it with sugar.

6. Use felt-tip pens to draw a mouth and eyes. Carefully fill in the nose.

Match the middle folds.

7. Put glue on the back of the head, but not on the nose. Press the head onto the blue paper.

8. Cut a rectangle of wrapping paper for a present. Glue it on below the head.

9. Cut two paws from white paper. Glue them on. Add claws with a black pen.

Tree and snowflake decorations

1. Fold a rectangle of green paper in half, long sides together.

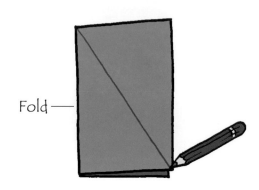

Fold —

2. Draw a line from the top of the fold to the opposite corner.

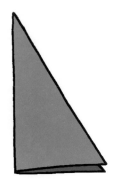

3. Cut along the line to make a tall triangle. Keep the paper folded.

4. Cut a triangle in the folded edge. Then, cut one in the other side.

5. Keep on cutting triangles in one side, then the other.

6. Carefully open out the tree shape and smooth the fold flat.

Snowflake

1. Use a pencil to draw around a mug on white paper. Cut out the circle.

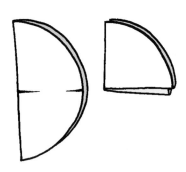

2. Fold the circle in half. Then, fold it in half again, like this.

3. Cut out small triangles from around the edges. Then, open it out.

Press small pieces of poster tack onto the tree and snowflakes. Press them onto a window.

Make lots of snowflakes and scatter them around the trees.

Glue on sequins or your own shiny stickers.

Reindeer wrapping paper

1. Use a crayon to draw the body. Add a neck.

2. Draw the head and add two ears.

3. Add four long legs and a tail.

4. Crayon hooves, a nose and two eyes.

5. Draw jagged antlers on its head.

6. Add spikes to the antlers. Fill in with pens.

Make a long thin card.

Make a gift tag to match the paper.

To draw a fir tree

1. Draw the trunk of a tree with a crayon.

2. Add branches with a light green crayon.

Draw lots of reindeer and trees on small pieces of paper. Then, glue them onto a large piece of bright wrapping paper.

3. Draw dark green branches over the top.

Tie some ribbon around your present.

Snowman paperchain

1. Lay two pieces of thin paper with their short sides together. Join them with tape.

2. Fold the paper in half. Then, fold it again so that the paper makes a zigzag shape.

3. Draw a snowman's hat at the top of the paper. Draw a head below the hat.

Don't cut along the folds.

4. Draw a band all the way across the paper. This will be the snowman's arms.

5. Add a big, round tummy. Draw in some fat legs. Add two feet to the legs.

6. Draw around the shape with a felt-tip pen. Cut it out along these lines.

7. Open out the shape. Fill in the hats and add faces. Decorate each one in a different way.

You can join your snowmen into one long chain and hang them up.

Christmas stockings

1. Fold a piece of paper as large as this page, in half, like this.

2. Use a pencil to draw a stocking shape against the fold.

3. Cut out the stocking, but don't cut along the folded edge.

Roll little pieces of tissue paper into balls and glue them on.

Draw shapes with glue and sprinkle on lots of glitter, or use glitter glue.

Tape on a loop of thread and hang the stockings on your Christmas tree.

Don't glue along the top.

4. Open the stocking Glue around one side, then fold the front over.

5. Rub your hand over the part you glued to flatten it.

6. Decorate your stocking using stickers, glitter and pens.

You could put a candy cane or a small chocolate bar inside each stocking.

You could decorate a stocking with stickers from the sticker pages in this book.

Advent calendar

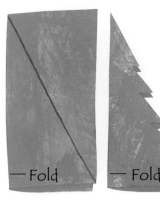

1. Cut a piece of bright cardboard or thick paper the same size as this book.

2. For the tree, fold a large rectangle of green paper in half, long sides together.

3. Draw a diagonal line, then cut along it. Cut out small triangles along the open edge.

—Fold   —Fold

You will need 24 altogether.

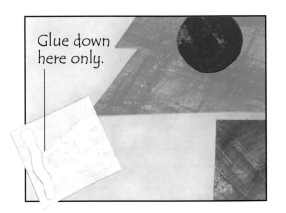

Glue down here only.

4. Cut a white shape for the snow. Glue it on. Open out the tree and glue it in the middle.

5. For the 'doors', draw different shapes. You could also use stickers from the sticker pages.

6. Cut out the shapes. Put glue along one edge of each shape and press it on.

Make sure your picture is smaller than the door.

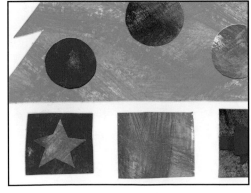

7. Draw a small Christmas picture behind each door, or press on a sticker.

8. Decorate the background with extra stickers and shapes cut from paper.

9. Use a felt-tip pen to write a number on each door. Start at one and go up to 24.

As you open each door during December, fold it back, so that it stays open.

Fingerprint fat robins

Dip your finger in paint each time you do a print.

1. Dip the end of one finger in brown paint. Print it onto paper. Do several more prints.

2. Dip a finger into red paint and press it onto each brown shape for a tummy.

3. Wash your hands. Dip a finger in white paint and print a spot inside the red shape.

4. Dip the edge of a piece of thin cardboard into brown paint and print two lines for the tail.

5. When the paint is completely dry, add a beak and eyes with a felt-tip pen.

6. Draw two wings and legs. For the feet, add three small lines at the end of each leg.

You could print robins on a piece of folded thick paper to make a Christmas card.

16

To..

Merry Christmas

from..

Merry Christmas

Tree card

Save this half for later.

Spread the paint with the back of a spoon.

1. Cut a big rectangle of thick paper or thin cardboard. Fold it in half, long sides together.

2. Get some help to cut a large potato in half from end to end. Cut one half into a tall triangle.

3. Lay some kitchen paper towels onto some old newspapers. Pour green paint on top.

Dip the potato into the paint each time you print a shape.

Add a sticker to the top of a tree.

4. Dip the potato into the paint and press it onto your card. Print more trees along the card.

Print a row of trees on bright paper.

5. Cut a square of potato. Dip it in red paint and print it below each tree.

Gift tags
Stars

You could write a name in the middle of the star.

1. Press the sharp edge of a star-shaped cookie cutter into half a potato. Press it in well.

2. Press the star into some thick paint, then press it onto thin cardboard.

3. Before the paint dries, sprinkle it with lots of glitter. Shake off any extra glitter.

4. Cut around the star, a little way away from the glitter. Tape ribbon on the back.

Snowmen

Small end

Big end

You don't need the middle piece.

Use pens to draw the face, hat and buttons.

1. Cut the ends off a carrot, so that you have a big end and a small one.

2. Dip the big end into thick paint. Press it onto thin cardboard, for a body.

3. Print a head with the small end. When it's dry, draw on a face, hat and buttons.

Round tags

Put the paint on an old plate.

1. Dip the edge of a piece of cardboard into gold paint. Print a criss-cross pattern on thin cardboard.

2. When the paint is dry, put a small lid onto the piece of cardboard and draw around it. Cut out the circle.

3. Use felt-tip pens to decorate the circle. Draw stripes and zigzags. Tape ribbon on the back.

Try drawing different faces on the snowman tags.

Wrapping paper

Make the slice as thick as your thumb.

1. You will need a cookie cutter and a potato, which is bigger than the cutter.

2. Cut a slice from the middle of the potato. Press the cookie cutter into the slice.

3. Push out the shape you have cut. You may need some help with the last two steps.

Try using gold or silver poster paint.

4. Dab both sides of the potato shape on some kitchen paper towels to dry it.

5. Press a fork into the shape. This will stop you from getting too messy when you print.

6. Pour two or three small patches of paint onto newspaper. Do them close together.

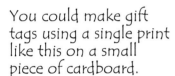
You could make gift tags using a single print like this on a small piece of cardboard.

7. Dip the shape into the middle of the paint, then press it onto a piece of paper.

8. Dip the shape into the paint again then print it. Fill the paper with printed shapes.

Use different shapes of cookie cutters together.

Christmas beads

Use a glue stick if you have one.

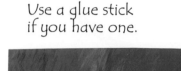

1. Cut a piece of wrapping paper as long as a fat straw. Make it the same height as your little finger.

2. Cover the back of the paper with glue. Lay the straw along one edge, then roll it up tightly in the paper.

3. Cover more straws with different wrapping papers. For a very long chain, you will need about five straws.

Use the beads to decorate branches or your Christmas tree.

Hang shiny decorations on the branches too.

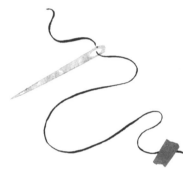

4. When the glue is dry, cut the straws into different sizes of beads. Cut some long and some short.

5. Thread a thick blunt needle with strong thread. Tape the long end of the thread to a work surface.

You could thread ordinary beads between your paper beads.

6. Thread on the beads until you have used them all. Put the needle through the last bead again and tie a knot. Do the same to the first bead.

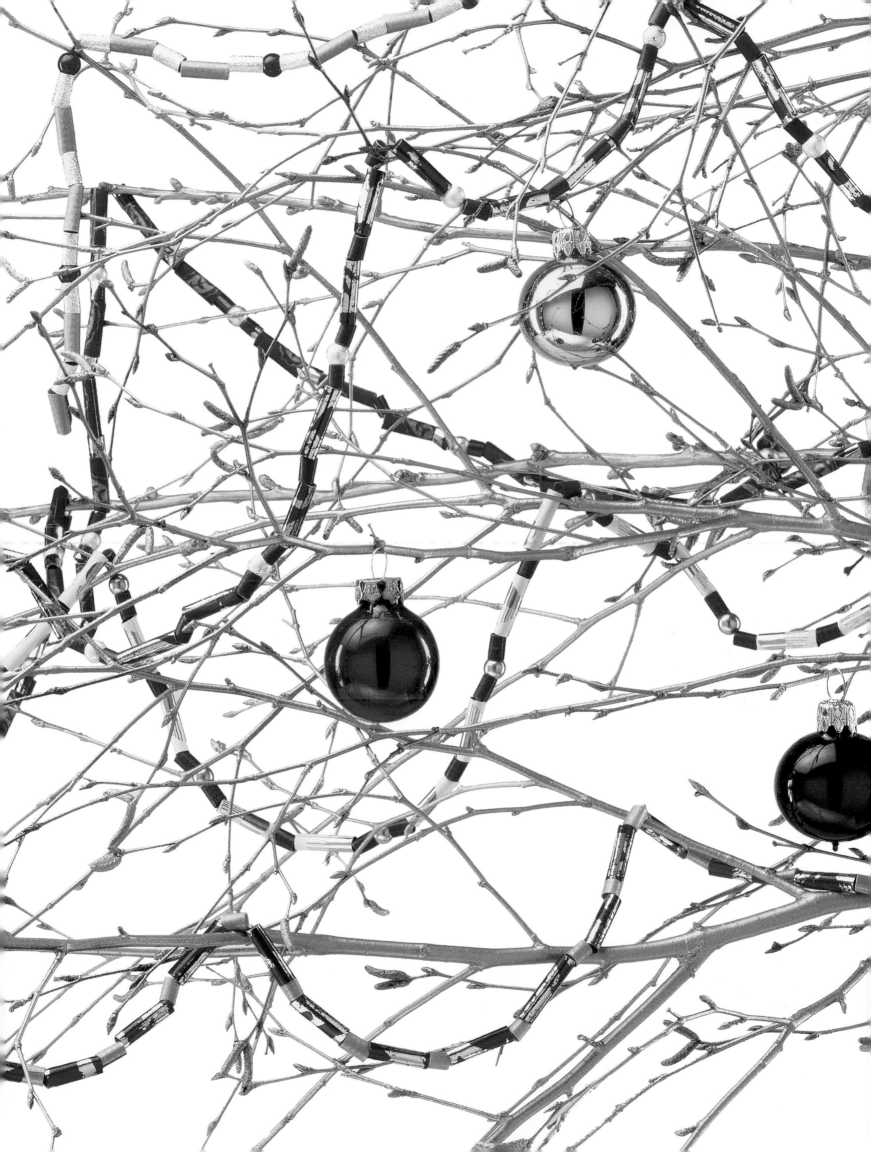

Paper angels

You could draw around a large coin.

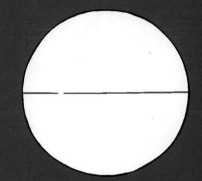

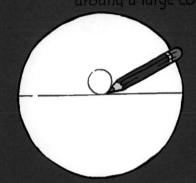

1. Put a plate onto a piece of thick paper and use a pencil to draw around it.

2. Cut out the circle you have drawn. Then, draw a faint line across the middle of the circle.

3. For the head, draw a small circle in the middle of the big circle, just above the line, like this.

Cut along this line.

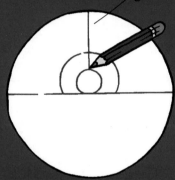

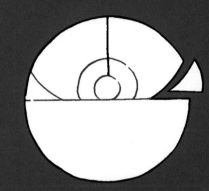

These will be the wings.

4. Draw a line around the circle. Then, draw a line from the edge to the head and cut along it.

5. Draw two curved lines, one on either side of the line across the middle. Cut out the shapes.

6. Draw four triangles around the edge, like this, then cut them out. These make the wings.

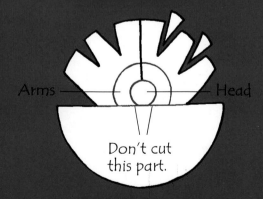

Arms — — Head

Don't cut this part.

7. Cut around the arms and the head, shown here in red. Don't cut through the neck.

8. Erase any pencil lines you can see. Then, fold the wings and the arms forward.

9. Decorate the angel with felt-tip pens, or draw shapes with glue and sprinkle them with glitter.

Use thick white or cream paper to make the angels.

Use gold paper or foil to make the halos.

Decorate the angels' skirts with stars and spirals.

10. Turn the angel around and bend the ends around to make a cone. Tape it together.

11. To make a halo, fold a piece of paper in half. Draw the shape shown here and cut it out.

12. Open out the halo and flatten the fold. Tape the halo to the back of the angel's head.

Use glitter glue, if you have it, to add dots to the angels' skirts.

Printed penguins

1. Make a pile of some kitchen paper towels on a thick layer of old newspapers.

2. Pour some black poster paint on top. Spread the paint with the back of a spoon.

3. Cut a big potato in half. Then, cut away two sides, like this, to make a handle.

4. To print a body, press the potato into the paint then press it onto a piece of thick paper.

5. When the paint has dried, use a smaller potato to print a white tummy on the penguin.

6. Dip a brush in a little orange paint and paint a pointed beak on one side of the penguin.

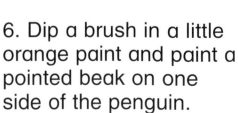

For a gift tag, cut around a penguin print, then tape ribbon to the back.

Make wrapping paper by printing penguins all over a large piece of paper.

7. Use a brush to paint a curved black flipper on each side of the penguin's body.

For a Christmas card, glue a printed penguin onto a piece of folded cardboard.

8. For the penguin's feet, paint two orange triangles at the bottom of the body.

9. Paint a white eye. Add a black dot to the middle of the eye when the paint is dry.

Handprinted angel

This is an
upside-down
dress.

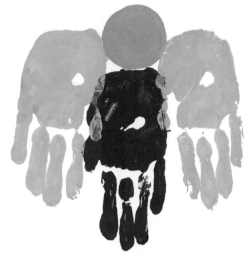

1. For the dress, press your hand in blue paint, then press it in the middle of some paper.

2. Press both hands into some yellow paint. Make two prints a little lower, for the wings.

3. Turn your paper. Dip your finger in pink paint. Go around and around, for a head.

4. Use your fingertip to do blue arms. Join them to the dress. Add some hands, too.

5. Use orange paint to finger paint some hair. Add a yellow halo above the head.

6. Dot on some eyes and a nose. Use your fingertip to paint a smiling mouth.

Fingerpaint lots
of stars around
your angel.

Glue your angel
picture to a piece
of stiff paper to
make a large
Christmas card.

29

Wrapping ideas
Spotted paper and tag

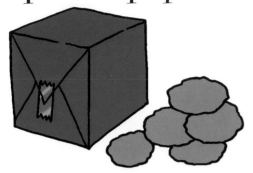  

1. Wrap your present. Then, rip lots of circles from a different piece of wrapping paper.

2. Glue the circles all over the wrapped present. Make them curve over the edges.

3. Rip lots of smaller circles from a different shade of paper. Glue them onto the circles.

Springy gift tags

 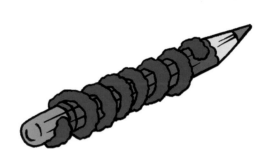 

1. Cut a star from thin cardboard. Decorate it with felt-tip pens, stickers or glitter.

2. Wind a pipe cleaner tightly around a pencil or felt-tip pen. Then, slide it off gently.

3. Push the last two coils of the pipe cleaner together at one end. Glue it to the back of the star.

4. Do the same to the coils at the other end. Put some glue on it and press it on your present.

Make a springy gift tag which matches your wrapping paper.

Tissue paper present

Press shiny star stickers onto each circle.

1. Cut a large square from a double layer of tissue paper. Lay your present in the middle.

Use tissue paper to wrap odd-shaped presents, such as a mug.

2. Gather the paper up around the present, then tie it with a piece of gift ribbon.

For a different springy tag, cut out a Christmas tree and decorate it with felt-tip pens or stickers.

Star card

Shake off the extra glitter when the glue is dry.

1. Draw three stars on a piece of bright paper and cut them out.

2. Put a blob of glue on each star and sprinkle it with glitter.

3. Cut three strips of thi paper. Glue a strip to th back of each star.

Cut out a tree shape. Make lots of stars and glue them on.

Glue under here.

4. Fold a piece of thick paper in half. Glue the stars onto it, like this.

5. When the glue is dry, stand the card up. The stars fall forward.

Tape a star onto a present. Write a name on it.